I0142834

SUCCESS WITH STRESS

JAE ELLARD

Stress is an important part of the natural world, aiding the natural selection and development of species. Simply put, the better species adapt to stress, the greater their odds of thriving and surviving. That said, the events that stressed us out as cave people are very different from the events that cause us stress in the modern world.

BEING ABLE TO COPE WITH AND NAVIGATE THE STRESS OF THE MODERN WORLD IMPACTS NOT ONLY OUR ABILITY TO THRIVE AS A SPECIES, BUT ALSO THE QUALITY OF THE LIFE WE LIVE.

WHAT IS

STRESS?

We all have experienced the feeling of being "stressed out," but what does being stressed out really mean?

The Merriam-Webster dictionary defines stress as a "constraining force or influence." Which makes sense— you can feel stressed when you feel restricted in some way.

Researchers know that just like balance, stress means different things to different people. What is stressful to you might not be stressful to your manager, coworkers, friends, or significant other. So it is important to remember that when it comes to defining stress, everybody has their own idea of what is acceptable, tolerable, and comfortable.

STRESS IS LINKED TO COMMUNICATION

— OR LACK OF IT.

WHERE DOES MODERN-DAY STRESS ORIGINATE?

MOST STRESS CAN BE TRACED TO COMMUNICATION—OR LACK OF IT—BACK TO THE CONVERSATIONS WE ARE NOT HAVING OR ARE TOO SCARED TO HAVE ABOUT WHAT WE VALUE, AND/OR A LACK OF BOUNDARIES TO PROTECT THOSE VALUES.

These could be conversations about our expectations, feelings, dreams, and desires, and expressions of how we want to fulfill them. It makes sense that at times we delay or avoid having these conversations because they can be scary and intimidating, as there is a certain level of emotional risk associated with these types of conversations.

Most commonly we respond to stress with three main emotions: anger, fear, or sadness. These emotions are also considered "masking" emotions that cover up deeper feelings of loss, grief, or distress.

These types of feelings can often be prevented by having clear communication about values and boundaries and the confidence and ability to express when these values and boundaries are not being upheld or respected.

WHAT CONVERSATIONS ARE YOU NOT HAVING?

WHAT FEELINGS ARE YOU NOT **EXPRESSING?**

To be realistic, **STRESS IS A PART OF LIFE AND THERE WILL ALWAYS BE TIMES OF STRESS.**

However, the level, duration, and frequency of stress is something **YOU DO HAVE THE POWER TO CHANGE.**

Now that you have an idea of what stresses you out, consider for a few moments what removing some of that stress in your life would look like.

WHAT WOULD LOWERING THE AMOUNT OF STRESS IN YOUR LIFE MAKE POSSIBLE?

PHYSIOLOGICAL STRESS

THE PHYSIOLOGICAL DEFINITION OF STRESS IS:

A specific response by the body to a stimulus that disturbs or interferes with the normal physiological equilibrium of an organism.

SIMPLY PUT, STRESS IS A NEGATIVE PHYSICAL, MENTAL, OR EMOTIONAL STRAIN OR TENSION THAT INTERFERES WITH YOUR NORMAL STATE OF BEING.

WHY & HOW

WE EXPERIENCE STRESS

Stress has its proper evolutionary place in our lives and that is to keep us alive when we are facing danger, such as being chased by a wild animal. If you were being chased by a wild animal, you'd experience something called "fight or flight" in which the physiology of your body would change in an effort to keep you alive.

"Fight or flight" is a concept attributed to Walter Cannon based on his research in biological physiology in the early 20th century that describes the response of the sympathetic nervous system (SNS) to perceived threats to emotional or physical security.

It wasn't until the 1950s that a man named Hans Selye popularized the concept of stress by theorizing that all individuals respond to all types of threatening situations in the same manner. This is when your SNS and your brain's hypothalamus take over the body and secrete into the bloodstream epinephrine ("adrenaline"), norepinephrine, and cortisol (also known as the stress hormone) to initiate the "fight or flight" response.

As this chemical reaction takes place, you might experience sweaty palms, a racing heart, and cold hands and feet as blood is directed away from the extremities to prepare for battle.

THIS PROCESS KEEPS YOU ALIVE IN THE FOLLOWING WAYS BY:

- causing a quick burst of energy

- increasing your hearing and sharpness of vision

- boosting your immunity

- decreasing your sensitivity to pain

- heightening mammalian brain functioning

THE THREAT IS GONE

NOW WHAT?

After the perceived threat has passed, it is very important that the body and brain move out of survival mode and to a relaxation response, so cortisol and adrenaline levels in the bloodstream can return to normal.

Research says it takes 40 to 60 minutes for the body to return to baseline body functioning. If the body and brain don't have the chance to relax, the result is a chronic stress state.

A CHRONIC STRESS STATE CAN:

+ decrease cognitive function (thinking and memory)

+ impair executive function (planning, deciding, troubleshooting)

+ impede motor skills

+ disrupt the immune system

+ disrupt sleep patterns

+ impede digestion

+ harm reproduction

+ stunt growth

THE IMPACT OF A CHRONIC STRESS STATE

When your body is trying to resume baseline body functioning, your parasympathetic nervous system (PNS) is working to chemically dilute the stress cocktail in your body to achieve homeostasis, or a state of metabolic equilibrium between the stimulating and the calming hormones in your body. When the calming doesn't occur, the brain continues to perceive stress. Even if there is no physical threat, your body can remain stressed. This type of sustained chronic stress can lead to serious, even life-threatening health issues.

SERIOUS STRESS-RELATED HEALTH ISSUES INCLUDE
BUT ARE NOT LIMITED TO:

- high blood pressure

- heart disease

- anxiety

- depression

- weight gain

- irritable bowel syndrome

- ulcers/acid reflux/heartburn

- decreased immunity

- sleep problems

CHANGE YOUR PATH

There must be as many strategies for managing stress as there are people on the planet. We each have developed our own workaround and ways to soothe ourselves when things really get spinning.

Sometimes we don't know what we don't know about healthy, sustainable ways to manage stress. That, paired with the notion that as humans we tend to make things more complicated than they need to be, makes it easy to understand why managing stress can be difficult.

5 STRATEGIES FOR SUCCESS WITH STRESS

YOU HAVE THE POWER RIGHT NOW to change the state of stress for yourself, your company, your family, your community, and even your country by cultivating new skills to manage stress with greater success.

GET CLEAR

GET CLEAR

An important key to managing stress is having clarity around how people, situations, and places make you feel and an understanding of your role. By creating this awareness, you can begin to accept the elements in your life that are truly causing you stress.

First determine if it is a person, place, or situation that is causing your stress, then open up to accepting accountability and get clear around your part, by considering how are you are acting and what you can do to minimize the negative feelings you are having.

1 2 3 4 5
GET CLEAR

By developing clarity around how you show up, and what conversations you are not having, you can begin to see how you contribute to these feelings, situations, and spaces.

WITH BETTER UNDERSTANDING OF THE ROOT OF YOUR STRESS AND YOUR ROLE IN IT, YOU CAN MORE CLEARLY SEE THAT YOU HAVE CHOICE IN HOW, WHERE, AND WITH WHOM YOU LIVE YOUR LIFE.

ARE YOU CLEAR ABOUT WHAT PEOPLE, SITUATIONS,
AND PLACES CAUSE YOU TO FEEL STRESSED?

ARE YOU CLEAR ABOUT HOW THESE PEOPLE, SITUATIONS, AND PLACES MAKE YOU FEEL?

GIVE UP CONTROL

FOCUS YOUR ATTENTION TO WHAT YOU CAN CONTROL: YOUR THOUGHTS AND ACTIONS AND HOW YOU RESPOND TO PEOPLE, PLACES, AND SITUATIONS.

The only thing you can truly control in life is you. You control how you feel, what you say to yourself (the little voice in your head), what you say to others, what you think, what you do, and how you respond to people and situations. Each day you have full control over every choice you make.

WHEN YOU SHIFT YOUR FOCUS AND AWARENESS TO WHAT YOU CAN CONTROL (YOU) AND RELEASE YOUR FOCUS ON CONTROLLING OTHER PEOPLE OR SITUATIONS, YOU WILL DRASTICALLY REDUCE THE LEVEL OF STRESS IN YOUR LIFE.

It is very common for us to try to control situations and other people to prevent change and protect ourselves from the unknown.

Every day you have the choice to either respond or react to a variety of different people and situations. Responding is grounded in thoughtful expression of your feelings; reacting is grounded in judgment and critique of others' actions or words.

WHEN YOU RESPOND,

YOU HONOR YOURSELF;

WHEN YOU REACT,

IT ELEVATES ANXIETY AND UNDERMINES YOUR PERSONAL POWER.

The most common ways people try to control or manipulate each other are by being passive-aggressive, guilting and shaming (through judgment and criticism), and in some cases being outright angry or aggressive. Using these reactive tactics and trying to control people and situations is as much of a choice as responding and focusing on expressing your feelings, needs, and boundaries.

When you approach people, situations, and change with mental and emotional stability and composure, or equanimity, a layer of stress in your life will melt away.

IS THERE A PERSON OR SITUATION **IN YOUR LIFE THAT YOU ARE TRYING TO CONTROL?**

WHEN EXPERIENCING STRESS, DO YOU REACT OR DO YOU RESPOND?

SAY WHAT YOU MEAN

SAY WHAT YOU MEAN

MANY TIMES WE CREATE OUR OWN STRESS BY SAYING THINGS WE DON'T MEAN, OR AGREEING TO THINGS THAT WE HAVE NO INTENTION OF DOING.

This is called hedging, and it often consists of using phrases like "I don't know," "maybe," and "we'll see," when you know your answer but have some fear around stating your true intention. When you hedge, you not only create more work for yourself in the long run to set the record straight, you cause stress for yourself in having to deal with the situation longer than necessary.

SAY WHAT YOU MEAN

When it comes to communication, the key to reducing stress is to be authentic—say what you mean and mean what you say. Not doing so can create false expectations in the person or people you are communicating with and needlessly create stressful situations.

This also includes your ability to communicate your boundaries. PEOPLE ARE NOT MIND READERS: unless you share with them what you like, what you don't like, and what is comfortable and tolerable to you, they do not know. You can prevent many stressful situations from happening by CLEARLY COMMUNICATING YOUR BOUNDARIES and setting expectations for how you want to be treated.

HOW OFTEN DO YOU USE HEDGING WORDS?

WHAT IS PREVENTING YOU FROM SPEAKING YOUR TRUTH?

HONOR YOURSELF AND OTHERS

1 2 3 **4** 5

HONOR YOURSELF AND OTHERS

There are two levels of compassion that correlate to stress. At the most basic level there is COMPASSION FOR SELF: how you treat yourself and your body, including the conversations you have with your inner critic. When you are kind to yourself, take care of your needs, and nurture yourself, you might find you are better able to manage stress.

Then there is THE COMPASSION YOU HAVE FOR OTHERS: how you value people's needs, emotions, and opinions. When you have awareness and respect regarding what is important to those around you and have clarity around others' values, goals, and points of view, they are more likely to respect and support you living your values, reaching your goals, and expressing your point of view. What's more, relationships with a higher level of empathy and compassion tend to have less tension because you are invested in each other's successes and failures, and are living the old adage, "Do unto others as you would have them do unto you."

HONOR YOURSELF AND OTHERS

By cultivating deeper compassion for the people in your life, in and out of work, you have the opportunity to reduce the level of stress you have that is generated from intolerance or impatience. When you move to compassion, you will find you ask more questions and make fewer assumptions and that you have a renewed level of patience around what a person is saying or why they are acting a certain way.

It is quite possible that by developing deeper compassion for yourself and others, the need to control outcomes will decrease as you become more open to accepting and respecting differing opinions, points of view, and ways of being.

DO YOU TREAT YOURSELF WITH COMPASSION?

DO YOU TREAT OTHERS **WITH COMPASSION?**

BE IN THE MOMENT

BE IN THE MOMENT

Another strategy to reduce the level of stress in your life is by MAKING THE CHOICE TO BE IN THE MOMENT YOU ARE IN and doing away with multitasking. Several research studies have shown that multitasking actually makes us less productive because it divides attention, therefore decreasing the quality of work and quality of experience. If you stop trying to do two (or more) things at once, odds are you might enjoy what you are doing more and have fewer tasks you need to follow up on later, thus reducing the level of stress you feel when you are doing too many things or managing too many conversations at once.

BE IN THE MOMENT

More important than being in the moment is having the ability TO BE IN NO MOMENT AT ALL, and allowing your mind the opportunity to not think, problem solve, ruminate, or make lists, but rather be still and at rest.

This skill can be thought of as concentration, meditation, or daydreaming; whatever you call it, over 250 universities have conducted nearly 1,000 studies on the benefits of doing it and research shows that it helps DEVELOP THE BRAIN, INCREASE CREATIVITY AND INTELLIGENCE, AND IMPROVE PROBLEM-SOLVING AND DECISION-MAKING ABILITIES. Research has also shown that actively emptying the mind on a regular basis reduces stress and stress-related disorders.

Creating nonthinking time is one of the best ways to reduce stress and recharge your brain at the same time.

DOES MULTITASKING **WORK FOR YOU?**

ARE YOU ABLE TO BE IN THE MOMENT?

OWN
IT.

GET CLEAR.

GIVE UP CONTROL.

SAY WHAT YOU MEAN.

HONOR YOURSELF AND OTHERS.

BE IN THE MOMENT.

Be confident in what you know about yourself and in the knowledge that the choice is yours regarding how you show up and how you respond to stressful situations.

THE CHOICE IS YOURS.

In 2008, Jae Ellard founded Simple Intentions, a company dedicated to developing employee awareness and publishing conscious content. In 2010, Jae authored the Mindful Life Program designed to help people disrupt patterns that cause imbalance and disengagement. To date, Jae's work has touched thousands of employees at multinational corporations in more than 50 countries spanning from Asia Pacific to Latin American, Western and Central Europe, Middle East, as well as Canada the United States. Jae has an extensive background in writing and communication with a master's degree in Communication Management from Colorado State University and a bachelor's degree in Broadcast Communication from Metropolitan State College of Denver. As a lifelong learner her passion has propelled her deep into research on human behavior, neuroscience, mindfulness, and organizational relationship systems. Jae writes columns and speaks on mindfulness in the workplace and is the author of seven books.

OTHER BOOKS BY JAE ELLARD

The Pocket Coach: Perspective When You Need Some is
a book of questions to help you make clear choices.

The Five Truths About Work-Life Balance is about the myths,
misconceptions and choices available to you to create
balance.

THE MINDFUL LIFE COLLECTION

STOP & Think: Creating New Awareness is about the choices
you have and the understanding of the impact of the choices
you make.

STOP & See: Developing Intentional Habits is about your
ability to consciously choose to create habits that support
your definitions of balance and success.

STOP & Listen: Practicing Presence is about working with your
choices to create deeper engagement with self, others, and
your environment.

Beyond Tips & Tricks: Mindful Management is about leading
groups to take accountability for making and accepting
choices.

Written by Jae Ellard

Edited by Jenifer Kooiman

Designed by Hannah Wygal

ISBN-13: 978-0986238727

ISBN-10: 0986238727

Success With Stress, 1st edition

2015 Copyright by Simple Intentions Inc.

This book may be ordered directly through the publisher at www.simpleintentions.com.

Contact: Simple Intentions, Inc., www.simpleintentions.com.
Simple Intentions creates conscious content to generate intentional conversations.

www.ingramcontent.com/pod-product-compliance
Lightning Source LLC
LaVergne TN
LVHW051354080426
835509LV00020BB/3423